HIRST

for

BENEDICT STELLA LUCY BARNEY

Nirgends, Gelieble,
wird welt sein,
als innen.

(There's nowhere, my love,
the world can exist
but within.)

Rainer Maria Rilke,
Duino Elegies (The Seventh Elegy)

THIRST

Michael
Woodward

P³P

Published in Great Britain 2001
THREE PEAKS PRESS
9 Croesonen Road
Abergavenny
Monmouthshire NP7 6AE
mail@p3p.org http://p3p.org

Designed & set in Joanna at Three Peaks Press

Printed in Wales at Gwasg Dinefwr, Llandybie

A CIP record for this publication
is available from the British Library

ISBN 1–902093–04–6

Contents

Dark and Light

Acknowledgements

Some of these poems have appeared in periodicals including *The Merton Journal*, *Scintilla*, *Spirituality* and *The Tablet*, and in the anthologies *Of Sawn Grain*, and *Private People* published by The Collective Press.

Thanks are due to Andy Berryman and all at the Collective Press and Scriveners for their early encouragement and to those who have read, listened and responded, especially Margaret who died before this book emerged.

Preface

I FIRST MET MICHAEL WOODWARD when I was invited to be a member of the interviewing panel for a position he had applied for. Michael was not successful and it fell to me to offer him a debriefing. It is a mark of who he is that at the end of the debriefing we were exchanging addresses and telephone numbers. We have been friends ever since.

If the voice of the poet is to be authentic then it has to speak out of a depth and integrity which is rarely allowed to be heard in our quick fix, consumerist society. And yet how little we seem to realise that our souls need the refreshing and provocative insights of the poet who reminds us of our vulnerability and deepest human potential.

In this new collection of poems Michael once again opens himself and his experiences to us in that unique way which allows his stories to be our stories too. He reminds us of our hopes and dreams, of our brokenness and our engagement with all of life's emotions. Ultimately he enables us to rediscover what it is simply to be.

I have regularly published Michael's poems in *The Merton Journal*, where they have found an appreciative audience. Readers recognise the voice of a fellow traveller who has the unique ability through his words to speak to us all in a personal and evocative way.

One of the strengths of the poetry is that you want to return to it again and again, as there is so much to be gained by each reading. In welcoming this new collection, I recognise that in Michael we have a strong, talented and distinctive poetic voice for our time.

Danny Sullivan
Editor, *The Merton Journal*

Calcutta Kitchen

THE KITCHEN at night
Was another place.

The moonlight glinting
On the upturned cruelty
Of the knife blade
Sitting squat on the floor,
Like a trap laid
For the unwary.

The hollow, rusty
Scuttle of cockroaches
Fleeing before my dusty feet.

Inside the hum
Of the fridge
Stood a shrine
Of brimful bottles

Trickled with beads,
A cool, misted breath
Of condensation on their glass

And within each one
The clear iced silk
I sought to heal
My seared and sleepless throat.

Starting Out

THE HARBOUR slowly dwindles
As our prow drifts on
Into the slate grey sea.

Ropes are coiled ready.
Our drill is crisp.
Sails hang, empty.

Where we will go
Depends on where
The wind comes from.

Exposed

Up the scarp of the valley
The wind boomed, evicting
Breath from our lungs,
Force-feeding us in gulps.
Gusts whetted on the granite
Knifed through four layers,
Granulating my marrow.

The ridge was ice
Beneath our unwelcome feet.
The wind came from everywhere.
North and south swam together:
My brain could not phrase a map,
Could only cling to its anchors
In my skull.

A hat tore loose
And soared like a lark,
Then plummeted beyond the drop.
We were humbled to our knees;
Stuck crab-like to the rocks,
Exhausted by the flap
Of collar, strap and sleeve.

Then overhead we saw
A mute Tornado,
Shocking in its silence.
It disappeared
With nothing to say above us
Engulfed within that rancour.

Words

WHEN DAY is done
All we have is words
Against the press of silence:
Wands to bend into fences,
Ploughs or bridges;
The intricate traceries
Of kin and clan
That repel, shelter
And embrace.

Words do not stay
But vanish in the night.
Paper holds them less well
Than our memory of a room
Stale with exhaled breath;
The sense of something shared
That we almost always miss
When the cup is empty,
The table swept.

Wind

THE GALE scythed
Through bough and trunk;
Torsioned branches cracked apart.

Parched earth furred with dust
Was spattered with drops
That beaded into rivulets.

My rigid tongue curled;
Its stale ligament loosened
As the wind uttered healing rain.

Histories and Legends

I can offer you neither honours nor wages;
I offer you hunger, thirst, forced marches,
battles and death.

Garibaldi

Alexander Meets Bucephalas

I SAW it happen.
My father groomed the horse after:
A huge magnificence of muscle
That quivered at a touch,
His eye like a storm breaking.

No man could subdue him
And so he roamed unridden,
Until the boy claimed him
In front of King Philip's cavalry.

He'd watched the royal trainer
Dumped in the dust and noticed his mistakes.
I felt that boy's grip.
Even then there was iron in his grasp
And he could halt a gallop with his will.
But he divined this was not a horse to master with iron,
Sensed it was remembered beatings that made him
Pummel the air with hooves.

The King had turned to leave the muster in disgust
When Alexander cried out the horse was his.
Silence.
            We thought he'd gone too far.
Philip wore a volcanic scowl,
But then seemed to think
This horse could teach his impossible son a lesson,
Motioned him on.

Alexander the grey, the white, the golden
Stepped up beside the pawing blackness.
He circled round to face the sun
Sparing him his shadow,
And let the bridle slip.

The unbroken touched the unbroken.
That tiny boy looked him in the eye
And spoke soft and low in Macedonian
A full turn of the glass
Before he swung up on his mane.

He sat astride still as marble,
Straight as a sarissa.
We who watched held our breath
And disbelieved our eyes.

A twitch on the rein
And they were gone to the river,
Flowing through the grass like a single creature,
Swifter than a hunting dog.

The King stood rooted as the cheering rang.
When they returned we knew
We had seen a horse without compare
And on his back
Our destiny, a god.

Skenfrith

CHARRED WOOD.
The reek of stale smoke.
All that's left
Of what was once
A village
Scattered round the mill
So carefully spared.

The motte is rising
Day by day,
Above the corpses
Of the slashed and hacked
Who ploughed, sowed and reaped
Crop and child here
For uncounted moons
Until the night this one near full was new,
And they stood and fell
When the horsemen came
With mail, sword, axe and torch.

By day the valley slopes echo
The sound of hammering,
The new wave of guttural vowels
And learn to absorb these too.

In the forest
The few who fled
Tire of their resenting watch.
They turn their backs
And seek the dark mountains,
Stacked like grievances
In the far distance.

Above what had been theirs
The rich banners
Hang limp and still,
Soaked by the alien rain.

1277

EDWARD SWAGGERED back to London
With the sacred totem
Of his subjugates,
Dewi Sant's skull,
Buried in his baggage-train.

Edward showed it off to London;
Then it disappeared from view.
A very Saxon thing to do
With the ivory of a people's pride:
Longshanks saw it; took it; lost it.

Llyn y Fan Fach: *A Welsh Legend*

A WOMAN like the wind
Outside the black church.

Above the bowed grief,
The sobs breaking
The crumpled silence,
She throws back her head,
Hair streaming,
And pours out laughter.

Osiris in the Usk

THE SURFACE of the Usk
Like flat broken glass.
A sinew quietly
Rippling beneath
Its pewter skin.

Moonstruck serpent
Clad in scuffed
Luminous silk
Weaving endlessly,
Languid, fluid.

Torrent of anger:
Libation, haemorrhaging
Brown tentacles
That lick ferociously
Round cattle and trees.

Usk's guts spread wide
Across the meadows,
Its waters still.
A fertile desolation:
Hara-kiri in the valley.

Beneath this desert
The silt is at work.
Swollen carcasses
Burn in sacrifice
Like Orion's stars.

Bryn Arw

BEACHED ON the emerald strand,
Some giant's upturned ship,
Rammed down, abandoned
And overgrown.

Smooth, slim splinter of rock.
What force slid you beneath
This floodplain's pastured skin,
A sore-red lesion
In the soft flesh of the valley?

This rusting hulk leaks
From secret springs.
Tautly sheathed in bracken,
Her russet hues at sunset
Unmatched by any palette.

Akhmatova

THEY BEAT her up
And called her names.

Night and day
The Neva flowed

Broken-nosed
Nun or whore,
She outfaced
Her tormentors,
Mourned her son.

Day and night
The Neva flowed

She lived her
Exile, endured
That silver age
Iced with menace.

Night and day
The Neva flowed

She sought her double,
Listened to her
Silent chorus;

Day and night
The Neva flowed

Carved their requiem
In blood
On paper skin,
With broken bone.

Night and day
The Neva flowed

Ice Man

YOU SEEM tenuous and brittle as a dry
Stick insect
But even after five thousand years
Your sinews
Hold you obstinately together.

So much you have to teach us. Just
Being there
You turn our arrogant nomenclature
Of time
Upside down. You can't be clutching your
Copper axe;
But, foolishly, we see you are.

You humble us with your grasp
And use
Of eighteen different kinds of wood;
The way
You took grass, sinew, feather, flint
And bark,
Threading them into your confident life.

You tease us:
Lying down where our borders disappear;
So both
Austria and Italy argued you their own.
They nearly
Rent you down the middle to be fair.

We sift
Your every crevice, sieve your secrets;
Finding even
What you had for your final meal; where
You lived;
What your nails had lately worked upon.

You are
Our countryman and brother, come to ask
Why we
In five thousand years between, and despite
The lives
Of prophets, sages, Gautama and Christ,
Have learned
To love less ourselves, our world and each other.

We muster
Information, detailed information
In answer
But we cannot penetrate your silence.
You tell us
We are tiny in the immensity
Of ice.

Meeting Tensing

Darjeeling, 1982

A DAPPER, ordinary man,
Neat; one who might wear
Slippers round the house
And snooze in a favourite chair.

He wore a white cap
As if this was Eastbourne
And he was going out
For an afternoon of bowls.

There in front of me stood
The one, among all of us,
The first to breach our frontier
With the breathless sky.

An aura clung to him still
In that after-dinner time of life
When I met Tensing,
Shook his hand;
Felt history in my callow palm.

The Coming of Saint Columba

Between the white manes
On the waves' backs
A coracle calmly bludgeons the swell,
Carving its thin wake
Towards a hard green place.

The Godspell it bears
Sealed in a cask,
Scribed in his own hand.

Tribesmen point and stare,
Then sprint to tell their elders
Of this tattered speck of sail
Swollen by a fair wind
Growing bigger,
Trailing a pennant of gulls.

Note: A painting by McTaggart with the same title hangs in the National Gallery of Scotland.

Intimations of Mortality

There is nothing stable in this world;
uproar's your only music.

John Keats, Letter
(to George & Georgiana Keats, 1818)

Early Lawns

When the twilight thickened
And the darkness
Rose in a mist
From the grass
The birds were silenced
Stillness spread around us
Like a blanket.

I remember those evenings
We didn't want
To end our games
Or go to bed,
Darkly playing on into the night:
And how I wondered
When I touched it
That the earth had grown so cold.

Saturday Matinee

THE MAJESTIC, South Woodford.
Red velvet seats
Gold braided curtains;
Where I stirred to be a poet,
Aged nine.

I was on my own.
Ring of Bright Water, half-empty.
The bit where the otter scuttles
Down the trench and gets
Chopped in two by the blade.

I cried, but it wasn't that.
Two lads, three rows in front
Turned and pointed and mocked me.
And I thought,
The bloody otter.

Bardsey Island, 1969

TOO YOUNG, back then,
To know the meaning
Of what I looked upon
But I remember Bardsey.

At the tip of Lleyn
We sat among sheep pellets
On the sweet turf,
Facing Ireland
And the faltering sun.

Someone spoke
But I lost the voice
Out on the glittering sound.

I was filled
By that thin green smudge
Sculpted from the haze;

Heard only
The tang of silver
Petalling the waves.

Fever

I REMEMBER that night
When fever gripped me tight
In a mad, black, throttling grasp,
Searing my veins with frenzy
Blind, prehistoric fear annihilating my metaphysics.

I remember that night
I lay, my guts strung tight
With vomiting, on a surrealistic nightmare
Ride to hell, more real than waking
Sharper than the needle that rescued me.

I remember that night,
My craving for dawn's light,
The weeks in bed but shudder no longer.
Pain's fangs are drawn by time, and I have learned
What it can mean, just to sit in the sun.

Somewhere Else

MY FATHER died at Mudeford Quay;
Clutching the bow of his dinghy,
Mun said. His pride and joy,
A snub-nosed *Mirror* it was:
His retirement toy.
He died alone. His bilge-boy,
The crew he trusted even with the tiller,
Was away; camped on Lleyn.
Not till the night I knew.

The sails flapped
Rigging creaked;
The wind howled.

Summoned to see the leaders
Late at night, I went slowly;
Expecting trouble:
I hadn't smoked at camp
But I could think of plenty
To be summoned for.
"Wasn't only me," I rehearsed;
"Can't say who," wondering if I could
Take it like a man.

The canvas flapped,
Guy-ropes creaked;
The wind howled.

"Bad news from home," he said
And instantly I knew
It was my father
Before he said another word.
Fog became my weather.
I took in he was dead,

But they wanted me to stay
And finish the camp;
Not go to his funeral.

The canvas flapped,
Guy-ropes creaked;
The wind howled.

I could have stayed that night
To nurse my griefs in big square tents,
Among consoling adults.
But I trudged back to my bell-tent,
Sleeping-bag; and sleeping friends.
The moon was a ghastly galleon
Plunging above the tump.
I had been boarded in the dark,
My dad untimely robbed.

The sails flapped
Rigging creaked;
The wind howled.

I lay awake; heard snores; could not cry.

Scenes from a Marriage

Ce sont les grands feux qui s'enflamment au vent,
mays les petitz s'esteignent si on ne les y porte au couvert.

(Big fires burn brighter in the wind, but little ones
die out unless they are sheltered.)

Francis de Sales, *Introduction à la vie dévote*

We become what we love.

Traditional

Spring

As soon as winter yields,
Print the snow
Thawing in the pass
With your mare's hooves,
And come to me.

I have here logs to burn,
But I shall be cold
Until I smell woodsmoke
From this fire
On your cloak.

Epithalamium

For Fleur and Patrick

2.11.96

YOUR FRIENDS left what they were busy doing and being,
And came from everywhere
To a gap in the magnolia chalk downs
On a raw November day
To celebrate your new beginning.

It was good to be there in Lewes,
To witness what you pledged.
Apt, too, for you to choose St Pancras:
Patron saint of journeys north and south,
And all our coming and our going.

We saw the expected result.
England 1, Zambia 1: a tie.
But with the wedding prayers said,
The wine drunk and the guests departed,
The match has now begun.

Our blessings, then, remain,
From every corner of the world;
What was one land is now five painful continents,
Floating and grinding on their plates:
We give you one for each.

That you, English oak and African baobab,
Grafted to a new creation
In front of our approving gaze
Will fit together, mutually creviced,
A parable of that first continent restored.

That you will give shelter
Each to each, and to others,

Aristocrat or *anawim*,
Known and unknown,
But foremost to yourselves.

That you will keep the spark
That's kindled by dear flesh:
The look across a crowded room
Which says, "you move me,"
And be patient when the fire flags.

That you will forgive,
And understand each other
When you can,
And understand that you won't
Always understand, or always love.

That you will flower together,
English oak and African baobab,
Above strong roots
And build unheard of bridges,
And share with us your fruits.

The Ring

YOU HOLD me
I warm.

You touch me
I flower.

You listen
I speak.

You love me
I sing.

Lune de Miel, Champtercier

For Monsieur Esmiol

OUR FIRST morning.
Marooned in our
Converted barn. Rain,
Day-long, relentless.

That afternoon
Our farmer knocked,
Diffident and soaked,
Bearing precious gifts.

A bulging bag of
Apples, plums, tomatoes.
Our recompense was
Only broken French.

Laying Down

WHY IS it that
Banishment to your cot
Lights your fuse?

I'd give anything
For three hours on,
Two hours off.
I'd take my blanket
Like a lamb.

You writhe and squirm
Rigid with indignation;
Ready to call Childline
On your push button
Fisher-Price mobile.

You don't shrink from me
When I scoop you
Later from the sheet
And taste your warm,
Cudded breath.

Your puffy-eyed
Vacant stare
Is not resentful.

The fit seems wiped clean:
Is it all forgotten
When you wake?

Adults bear
The weight of memory.
I can't forget
How those desperate creases
Sealed your eyes.

Power of Speech

How you burbled and chortled:
And nothing came of it but dribbled
Spit. All of you was soggy then.

You cried for everything and nothing, it seemed,
Until you began to hum and cluck
And we flattered ourselves
That you meant "Dad" and "Mum."

Then your sisters taught you
The rudest words they knew;
And we had "bum" for a fortnight.

They tormented you with their adoration,
Helpless as you were then,
Marooned in a dry dock of muteness
Until you floated your first phrases:
"Stop it" and "Leave me alone."
I knew then my son's judgement was sound.

Now your sails have billowed
Full, and you can rig your own
Brilliant spinnakers of meaning
Whilst we are left, upturned in your wake.

Discovering Books

SMEAR OF sleep
Parted just enough
For me to furl one eyelid
And not quite focus
On a cheerful face
Thrusting into mine.

"Wake up, Dad," he said,
A book in each hand.

I protested.
He was implacable.

"You have to, Dad," he said.
A book in each ear
Persuaded me he was right.

The duvet lifted mechanically;
My arm curled him in.
But he was not content with warmth.
He burned for books,
And I was his kindling.

For My Wife

You are beautiful
With a beauty
Deeper than youth.
Now the warmth
Of holding you includes
The times we've held
Each other together, tenderly;
Cherishing the skin,
Knowing how fragile
We both are underneath.

The Paradox of Yield

It's funny how love starts out
With total and utter,
A winged forever
That knows no limits,
Ready to dance, sing and laugh in abandonment.

And love, if it can, slowly matures
Into scraping dog shit off the shoes,
Saying yes when you feel no
And staying put,
Growing roots quietly from a withering seed.

Just to Say

Forgive me if I'm thrilled with the idea,
but just now I thought that every poem
I write ought to be called Happiness.
Raymond Carver

MY CHILDREN'S cheeks
Are dimpled places
  Where I bury kisses.
Our young sophisticates
Brush such seeds away,
But I trust these crevices
  Will flower one day.

Dealing with my Hand

LIVED ABROAD,
Learned a bit,
Been thin and fat;
Done all that.

Skin sagging in places;
Won't say where.
Lines are carved now
Deeper than smile creases.
They don't go away.

Hair's abandoning ship;
Clings around the rafts
Of plug hole and pillow.
On board, the grey invaders
Will soon be winning
Against what's left.

Once played
Football, cricket, even rugby
After a fashion.

Found that inside us
Is the horizon
That matters;
Still trying to find
And share it.

Four kids sleeping upstairs
Leech money, time and love,
Nearly everything I have.
They're welcome.

One knuckle's humped to a ridge
From not catching that ball
In the nets.

This gold ring
Grips another finger tight,
Holds our lives together.

Exhumed centuries hence,
A few stray bones turned over
By some synthetic metal plough,
They might notice this worn groove
Above the joint

And wonder, like me,
What it all means.

Dark and Light

Nel mezzo del cammin di nostra vita
Ci retrovammo in una selva oscura
Che la diritta via era smarrita...

(Midway through the journey of our life
I found I had strayed into a wood so dark
That my way forward was utterly lost...)

Dante, *Inferno* (Canto One)

We have to be in a desert.
For he whom we must love is absent.

Simone Weil, *Gravity and Grace*

Comet in the Car

IT HUNG
Brilliant in the west,
Throbbing against the blue-black
Night; like a shower of rain
Pattering silently on the sky:
A renegade sun
Pursued by a clutch
Of clamouring planets.

It scalpelled my flesh
To wonder.
It seemed natural
To expect events rich and strange
In that wake,
See a portent in its dazzle.

I glimpsed it furtively at first
From my side window.
But when I swung out
On to the Raglan Road
It was overhead,
In the middle of my windscreen,
Crumbling its bread into the utter dark;
Making my way auspicious,
For a mile, at least.

Comet in the Garden

When I came home at ten
The girls were in bed,
Awake, and in trouble:
"They'll be fit for nothing to-morrow."

Unhelpfully, I called them down
In dressing-gowns.
They flopped excitedly into boots
And staggered outside in my wake,
Scraping bleary-eyed round the silent house.

In a gap between our sloping eaves
And the tall poplar across the road
We picked out the comet.

It was warm and sheltered there
But I hugged them both close.
"I want you to remember this," I said,
Before they skipped lightly off to bed;
And I made peace with my wife
Beneath the bright, disintegrating ice.

Canal Death

Like Ophelia
She is sunk in a deep sleep of peace
Legs poised to run,
Her stiffening body tricked out in weeds.
Her neck arched backward
Baring the palest throat.

Through misted waters
I can hear the silence
That engulfs her;
See the tight spiral
Of her double helix slackening,
Like plants unravelled in water.

Her wool begins to float away in lumps,
The prelude to her unmaking.

In the Cathedral

"What does it mean
To follow your Christ?"

How in the name of God
Can I preach Christ
To this pagan and unlettered boy?

"The window. See the colours.
Bright and daring. Is it not joy
To your senses, a feast?"

"It is."

"To follow Christ
Is to be such a window."

"I have no colours or letters.
I am not glass. I am not
Leaded into patterns that please.
Your Christ is for scholars,
And the gentle, not for me."

"Have you seen the window
After sunset? A dark nothing.
So we are. You and me.
All of us the same."

"Then I am but the lead."

"If you know that in your heart,
My son, you may indeed frame
A window for Christ to fill."

"What must I do?"

"Does the glass you see
Strive or clamour or wander?
The sun rises every day;
Do whatever you will.
Only let through the light."

Trip to Bakkhali

I

THE ANNUAL outing for school.
Everyone bound for Bakkhali,
Even the kitchen comes too.

Leaping children, eyes dancing;
Teachers quieter but yielding
Nothing in their gladness

To be forsaking desk and book
On this fine winter's dawn
For somewhere other.

No museum trip for us.
We take the Diamond Harbour Road
As far as it will go.

Ours a kind of pilgrimage:
We are pledged to discover
The mouth of the Ganges,
To learn all we can from the beach.

Winter sun bright but gentle;
The dust light, distances shimmering.

As we travel on beyond tarmac
India seems to be slowly sinking,
Shipping water beside our road.

Still fronds of palms shelter wayside shrines,
The dark, garlanded caves.

Traffic thins. Still we pass
The impossibly peopled buses
But now we see more of hooves than wheels.
The road ahead seems smooth.

II

Then Atul opened a wallet of *pan*.
A dozen lay there, carefully wrapped.
His dark lips closed around
A sleek, green, folded leaf.

The smell seduced me:
A quintessence of the streets
With the ordure decanted. I thought:
I am here; I will drink deep.

Atul's *pan* seemed the real thing,
Not the bland stuff of weddings:
This the kind I didn't know how to buy
At the roadside shacks.

When I asked for one I didn't read
Atul's friendly reticence,
Assumed we knew each other better,
That he would tell me truth.

I didn't catch his hospitable wish
Not to disappoint,
That tells the traveller
His sought for destination
Lies in whatever direction
That traveller most desires.

So it sat in my palm,
The cool green leaf aromatic,
Its deadliness disguised.

"*Jorda*," said Atul. And smiled.
Jorda: a new Bengali word.
Happy eating perhaps, I thought.

I missed the significance of nudges:
"Michael da: *Jorda pan!*"
I missed the neat tabacco, too, whilst
I savoured the lime, betel nut and seeds.
But it didn't miss me.

Soon the landscape had disappeared
And now the road ploughed through my gut.
We made our half-way stop.
I felt I was at my end. My Bengali
Friends got off. I couldn't move.

The stationary bus bucked and heaved.
I was an airsick pig. Colour throbbed
Between yellow, pink and brown.
My entrails rose and sank
Spewing chaos in my inner ear.

O the bliss
When the horizon levelled
And the colours matched.

We moved on.
I entered folklore as
Michael da of the *Jorda pan*.

III

India's leaks got worse. We drove
Along the salient above water
Deep enough to ripple with waves.

On through the savage denseness
Of the Sundarbans stacked on either hand,
Straining to catch a blaze of tigers in the green.
The children sang, as only Bengalis can.

We stopped for tea by an English church
Where the air tasted salt
And the wind sang through reeds.

Whilst the leaf, the sugar and the milk
Boiled up together in the kettle
We read runes in the cemetery,
Its stones foundations of the Raj.

The bald poignancy of words
Carved a hundred years ago
Spoke their stories to the wind:

How a girl from Liverpool
Came to join her sweetheart,
Sailed from home, aching to step ashore,

Boldly pledged to embrace Bengal.
But her ship went down a mile from shore
And she came to land a corpse.

IV

We drank our *chai*, and fortified
We squeezed aboard a ferry.
That stone affected me.
I checked how well the seams were caulked.

The ferry sagged with people. Oiled hair gleamed;
The afternoon sun caught the jewellery.
Saris flapped, bright as transparencies.
Red teeth clenched, the oarsmen pulled.

On the other side, India was sinking fast.
The road was ours. Nowhere to go
But to our beach. We were there at last.

Our hotel was star blessed.
The last building in India.
Salt-warped wood, nearly black,

Gave my walls heavenly cracks
Through which I could hear and see
The sky, the beach, the stars, the sea.
This was Bakkhali.

Epiphany at the Bay of Bengal

WORDS WON'T take you very near, my love,
But somehow I would have you know
How I have been transfigured.

Rapt and speechless on the seashore
I've sat many times before,
but this was otherwise.

Time melted:
I can't place when the world split open
And I fell inside.
One moment I was, as you know me,
Vague and moony and alone.
Then suddenly I saw, and knew
What I had only read before;
That all's one
And ripeness is all.

Hurt with awe
I loved and sang and cried
As the waves washed my feet in moonlight.
In that persistent moment
The whole world hung against my heart.
Sharp and beautiful,
It drove home deep inside me.
Once pierced, there's no forgetting.

Over and gone now,
But still the buried ache
Coaxes out a prayer
Never to be healed of that wound,
Or to relent from offering
The hard love that suffers into flower.

The Weather in Lhasa

In Lhasa
Women are put in prison,
Chained and beaten

For singing about
Dark clouds passing
In front of the sun

As they wash
Their clothes
In the river.

Remember them
When you wash your clothes
(Even if a machine does it for you);

When you see clouds
And talk of rain;

Remember them
Especially when you feel
The warmth of the sun.

Tibet

THESE CLOUDS will dissolve:
Prayer flags flapping in the wind,
Some older than Mao.

Forest Floor

I LAY on my back in the forest
The needled floor dry, and soft enough,
Eyes drawn upward to where three trees met.
In the sky beyond
The sun sulked behind clouds.

The clog of wood above weighed heavy.
The branched trunks
Were huge harrowing bars;
Vast tank flails freeze framed.

Where the three dark crowns merged,
The feathered needles burst
Into luminous transparent green
When the sun pulsed.

Another Welsh Landscape

To live in Wales is to be conscious
Of dissension.
Here we eat paradox for bread,
Share the arteries to everywhere
That stifle circulation;
Nurse a history lost,
A landscape burned in anger.
The valleys echo words
But they send nothing back the same.

The past is a wound.
Wales is sick to death
Of others' pride,
The endured pomp and tramp
Of Roman, Saxon, Norman, Saxon:
The moronic rhythm
That undermined the song,
Tore a tongue out at its root.

But there are relics real to faith;
Potency is here,
Tucked beyond
All the decayed winding-gear
Of the heart.
That howl you hear is birth;
The steaming viscera are placental.

Sometimes the rain lifts.
With the wind in the right quarter
You may catch
An old song making new.

The Cwm of Peace

For Victor and Esther

Standing here
Above the plunged scar
Worried out by water,
Nature's sharpest knife,
I feel like a maker
And something fashioned, too;
Another carving, incomplete.

Below,
The loud poured out torrent
Crashing on to granite
Underwrites the silence.
This is a place to pray.

The house sits
Calm as a buddha;
Two shells seamed in to one.
In the cool garden
A hearth's peace pitches its tent
Beneath the blackbirds
Jugging out their psalms.

In this place
Clean of human sound
You can trace the Cwm's silver thread
Along the sheer drop,
Through the stand of hazels
Switching your cheek;
Treading a slow, careful path
Towards the hill's heart.

A Postcard for Thomas Merton

AT FOURTH and Walnut today, it's just
Any old crowd milling: I guess it always was.
But you're there too among them, helping us remember.
And from these books you get under my skin,
Firing the ache for something whole and simple: the truth.

It's funny how the cheese and the conflicts
Don't matter now. There's so much cheese
We have to deal with. But you needed that, too:
It had its place in the mountain climb, one of many paths
Leading to the crossed roads of your heart.

I want to thank you for staying with them all; not going
Anywhere much: letting those roads worry you awake.
Smile on us then, reclining as you must now, at home
Among buddhas, saints and outcasts; their familiar.
And pray for blessing on our small wits,
And on our turbulent, distracted hearts.

Shepherd

It was a foul night:
Sharp, whetted cold,
Fog as thick as fleeces.
We sent the dogs demented
With our reek of sheep
As we stumbled into Bethlehem.

No messengers there to show us.
They only came once;
Left us the mystery.
But they had said truth:
It was the cave.
We had argued the child indoors
On our journey.
Such a night
Seemed too raw, too harsh
For childing in straw.

Long searching it took
To find the inn
We visited by day.
The streets were different in that fog.

But we knew it was the place
When the cave loomed
And we heard that cry
Pierce the dark.

We all remembered it as light
Because of the joy
That burst us all asunder in that cave,
But in truth
It was a foul night.

Nazarene

When you came up from the waters
There was no going back to carpentry.

Even then it was your hands that mattered:
Something other happened where they touched.

When you stretched out your weathered hands
Familiar with the work of wood and nails,

Everything changed. You changed everything:

Fasting in the desert
And drinking the outcast's wine;

Making whole the broken,
Breaking the healing bread;

Giving us your life and peace
Out of our agony.

He Must Wax

WHAT MAGNETIC pull caused my lads to up
And follow him? It was expected, yet
Awesome still. I saw how he looked at them.
"Come and see," he said. So they did; and stayed.

I scarcely saw them then, except to yield
Others from my dwindling band. Two days on
Was the Cana wedding. I didn't go.

When they came, incredulous, and told me
I knew that he had shown his hand. They bled
From me to him. I knew they would, one day.

He is the rising sun; our dawn breaking.
Now I can rest a while behind a cloud.
I am tired beyond words. Lord, these arms ache.
My work is finished.
I long for the desert.
Your will be done.

The Dark Sabbath

THIS DOG-DEAD day:
Time oozes stubbornly,
Like pus from a wound.
No wind stirs.

Behind our locked door
We, the hungry, cower
And sob in whispers,
Or say nothing at all.

In the street
Dogs with pinned ears
Pad round in circles,
Their tails trailing.

The air is heavy with grief.
I see Gennesaret,
Flat with a dead calm
That is not peace.

The sun sinks at last,
A coin mired in blood.
The women slip out.
No one ate today.
To-morrow we'll need food.

Crying stabs the dark.
In the night, a woman rises:
The reek of juniper and myrrh.
I hear the bolt grate.

Three figures creep past.
I turn back to the wall.
My heart is stone.

Being Lazarus

THESE CLOTHS are wound
Tight as thongs.
Movement is a memory.
My dry lips
Utter neither word nor song.

All is sealed tight.
The thick darkness stifles.
I do not know now
What is my flesh,
What the stone I lie upon.

Is this how our fathers sleep?
Do we come only
To this nothing
Where I lie empty;
Imagining a crowd outside,
An echo of my name?

Lazarus Raised

THE SHOCKING thing was how I smelt.
No wonder they shrank back.

I had been spared that on my slab.

The light was like the dark.
Still I couldn't see.

Slowly I began to sip colours.

Then there was the breeze
Like fingers on my flesh.

The questions pounded in my skull.

When I loosed my hold of him
The horizon was huge and empty.

Now

Now the silence
Is intense
With the embrace
Of the one
I have sought
For years
And only ever glimpsed.

In my battered,
Proud, dark
And ungrateful heart
Wakes the joy
Of having nothing
Between us,
No images or words,
Only the creating love
That I want always
To be the place
Where I live.

Nirmal Hriday

Literally means "Place of the Pure Heart".
It is the name of the Home for the Dying
in Calcutta, run by the Missionaries of Charity.

THE STENCH of excrement
Clenches my throat.
Metal bowls and mugs,
Scrubbed clean with ashes
And shreds of coconut,
Glint in the sunlight
That hangs in shafts.

In the morning, the van;
The night's wrapped corpses
Are lugged outside.
The sick fret and moan,
Or lie still, and smile.

The day is ordinary things:
Water, medicine, talk, washing.
The work of a worn threshold.
On the wall by the stove
Where the dhal bubbles
Is a simple cross
And two words: "I thirst."